Lawful Permanent Resident Parent Petitioning Child

Written by an Immigration Law Firm

Attorney Brian D. Lerner

LAW OFFICES OF
BRIAN D. LERNER
A PROFESSIONAL CORPORATION

Lawful Permanent Resident Parent Petitioning Child

Written by Attorney Brian D. Lerner
Copyright © 2022 by Immigration Law Offices of Brian D. Lerner, APC
All rights reserved.

Disclaimer and Terms of Use:

Effort has been made to ensure that the information in this book is accurate and complete. However, the author and the publisher do not warrant that this particular petition will mirror or be exactly as your situation. There has not been any attorney-client agreement created by the purchase of this petition or application. No legal advice has occurred. The cases, regulations and/or statutes cited may change at any time without notice.

Print ISBN: 978-1-948774-94-9
Ebook ISBN: 978-1-948774-93-2

INTRODUCTION

There are a multitude of different immigration petitions and applications. They are complex and full of requirements. Obviously it would be best to hire and immigration attorney to best prepare the petitions and application. However, this can certainly cost thousands of dollars.

The next best option is to get a sample of the petition written by an experienced immigration attorney. The samples cost a fraction what would be charged by an immigration attorney. However, while the reader has to alter, amend and change the parts of the sample petition to reflect their actual situation, it is a fantastic roadmap for them to use. If the reader has purchased the entire petition or application, they will have real live samples of cover letters, forms, declarations, affidavits and the necessary exhibits to use. The samples come from real cases and the names of those clients have been redacted to protect the privacy of that person or corporation.

These are petitions and applications that have been drafted by an experienced immigration attorney with over 25 years of experience. Get the benefits of that experience without the costs.

About the Law Offices of Brian D. Lerner

The Law Offices of Brian D. Lerner, APC. The law practice consists of Immigration and Nationality Law and everything involved with and regarding immigration which includes citizenship, investmet visas, family and employment visas, removal and deportation hearings, appeals, waivers, adjustment, consulate processing and all types of immigration and citizenship matters. Thousands of families have been reunited and/or permitted to stay in the U.S. and/or return to the U.S. because of the successful work of Immigration Attorney Brian D. Lerner.

This law offices handles all types of immigration cases including family based and employment based. Immigration issues range from immigration court proceedings to trying to fix what paralegals may have done that was neither correct nor proper. Foreign nationals must have experience lawyers admitted to practice law.

The Law Offices of Brian D. Lerner, APC, handles cases arising from business visas, work permits, Green Cards, non-immigrant visas, deportation, citizenship, appeals and all areas of immigration. The Law Offices of Brian D. Lerner, APC does EB-5 Investor Visas, H-1B Specialty Occupation, L-1 Intracompany Transferee, E-2 Treaty Investor, E-1 Treaty Trader, O-1 Extraordinary Ability among others. Regarding immigrant visas for the Green Card, the firm does PERM and advanced degree PERM, Family Petitions, and Extraordinary Alien Petitions. In addition to affirmative petitions, the Law Firm represents people in deportation and removal hearings, including political asylum, withholding of removal, and convention against torture cases.

Brian D. Lerner has been certified as an expert in Immigration & Nationality Law by the California State Bar, Board of Legal Specialization sicne 2000 and has been re-certified three times. He now passes on his decades of experience by allowing the Reader, Law Schools, Professors and other Immigration Attorneys to purchase sample petitions on every facet of Immigration Law.

TABLE OF CONTENTS

About the LPR Parent Petitioning Child

Are you a Lawful Permanent Resident and want to petition your single child who is under 21 years old? In this case, you have your Green Card and it will be considered a Second Preference Petition and you can move on to the next step the moment it becomes current to either adjusting status or consulate processing. The first part must be done and must be done properly in order to ever proceed to the next part. Without a proper I-130 application there will never be a Green Card. If approved, then you could move onto the next step in the Immigration process. If not approved, it will take years of red tape. You might be able to 'lock' your childs age in as younger than 21 as well. Remember, it is your responsibility to submit everything correctly. This sample I-130 Petition has everything necessary to give you the best chance possible to get an approval. Just input your own information and use the application as a guide. It has been prepared by an expert Immigration Attorney. Thus, this book will allow you to see a guide of how it is done, prepared and submitted.

SECTION 1:

Attorney Cover Letter

Law Offices of Brian D. Lerner

A PROFESSIONAL CORPORATION

CERTIFIED SPECIALIST IN IMMIGRATION AND NATIONALITY LAW
ADMITTED TO THE U.S. SUPREME COURT

LONG BEACH, CALIFORNIA
(562) 495-0554

CARSON, CALIFORNIA
(310) 884-9430

October 22, 2018

U.S. Citizenship and Immigration Services
Attn: I-130
PO Box 21700
Phoenix, AZ 85036

      RE: **I-130, Petition for Alien Relative**
              Petitioner: ███████████████████
              Beneficiary: ██████████████████

Dear Sir/Madam:

We hereby submit an I-130, Petition of Alien Relative, for ███████████████
(hereinafter "Petitioner") on behalf of his daughter ██████████████████ (hereinafter
"Beneficiary").

Enclosed herein please find the following documents:

FORMS

Form:	Description:
G-28	Notice of Entry of Appearance as Attorney or Accredited Representative (Petitioner); and
I-130	Petition for Alien Relative with $535.00 Filing Fee.

EXHIBITS

Exhibits:	Description:
1.	Copy of Petitioner's Birth Certificate with English Translation;
2.	Copy of Petitioner's Legal Permanent Resident;
3.	Copy of Beneficiary's Birth Certificate with English Translation;
4.	Copy of Beneficiary's Foreign Passport; and
5.	Copy of Petitioner's Marriage Certificate.

Under the Immigration and Nationality Act ("INA") § 201 (b) (2) (A) (i), the Immediate Relatives, including children, spouses and parents, of a U.S. citizen may be petitioned for an immigrant visa, without being subjected to direct numerical limitations.

In the present case, Petitioner is a U.S. Permanent Resident. Beneficiary is the daughter of Petitioner. Therefore, Petitioner is qualified to file an Alien Relative Petition on behalf of his daughter.

Based on the foregoing, we respectfully submit that the attached evidence shows the necessary relationship exists and that the instant I-130 should be approved.

Thank you for your consideration in this matter. Should you have any further questions, please feel free to contact our office at █████████.

Sincerely,

Attorney at Law

SECTION 2:

Forms

Notice of Entry of Appearance
as Attorney or Accredited Representative

Department of Homeland Security

DHS
Form G-28
OMB No. 1615-0105
Expires 05/31/2021

Part 1. Information About Attorney or Accredited Representative

1. USCIS Online Account Number (if any)

   ▶ [ ]

Name of Attorney or Accredited Representative

2.a. Family Name (Last Name) [████]

2.b. Given Name (First Name) [████]

2.c. Middle Name [████]

Address of Attorney or Accredited Representative

3.a. Street Number and Name [3233 E. Broadway]

3.b. ☐ Apt ☐ Ste. ☐ Flr. [ ]

3.c. City or Town [Long Beach]

3.d. State [CA] 3.e. ZIP Code [90803]

3.f. Province [ ]

3.g. Postal Code [ ]

3.h. Country [USA]

Contact Information of Attorney or Accredited Representative

4. Daytime Telephone Number [(562) 495-0554]

5. Mobile Telephone Number (if any) [ ]

6. Email Address (if any) [████]

7. Fax Number (if any) [(562) 608-8672]

Part 2. Eligibility Information for Attorney or Accredited Representative

Select all applicable items.

1.a. ☒ I am an attorney eligible to practice law in, and a member in good standing of, the bar of the highest courts of the following states, possessions, territories, commonwealths, or the District of Columbia. If you need extra space to complete this section, use the space provided in Part 6. Additional Information.

   Licensing Authority
   [**California Supreme Court**]

1.b. Bar Number (if applicable)
   [████]

1.c. I (select only one box) ☒ am not ☐ am subject to any order suspending, enjoining, restraining, disbarring, or otherwise restricting me in the practice of law. If you are subject to any orders, use the space provided in Part 6. Additional Information to provide an explanation.

1.d. Name of Law Firm or Organization (if applicable)
   [Law Offices of Brian D. Lerner, APC]

2.a. ☐ I am an accredited representative of the following qualified nonprofit religious, charitable, social service, or similar organization established in the United States and recognized by the Department of Justice in accordance with 8 CFR part 1292.

2.b. Name of Recognized Organization
   [ ]

2.c. Date of Accreditation (mm/dd/yyyy)
   [ ]

3. ☐ I am associated with
   [ ]
   the attorney or accredited representative of record who previously filed Form G-28 in this case, and my appearance as an attorney or accredited representative for a limited purpose is at his or her request.

4.a. ☐ I am a law student or law graduate working under the direct supervision of the attorney or accredited representative of record on this form in accordance with the requirements in 8 CFR 292.1(a)(2).

4.b. Name of Law Student or Law Graduate
   [ ]

Pg 5

Part 3. Notice of Appearance as Attorney or Accredited Representative

If you need extra space to complete this section, use the space provided in **Part 6. Additional Information.**

This appearance relates to immigration matters before (select **only one** box):

1.a. ☒ U.S. Citizenship and Immigration Services (USCIS)

1.b. List the form numbers or specific matter in which appearance is entered.

> I-130

2.a. ☐ U.S. Immigration and Customs Enforcement (ICE)

2.b. List the specific matter in which appearance is entered.

3.a. ☐ U.S. Customs and Border Protection (CBP)

3.b. List the specific matter in which appearance is entered.

4. Receipt Number (if any)
  ▶

5. I enter my appearance as an attorney or accredited representative at the request of the (select **only one** box):

☐ Applicant   ☒ Petitioner   ☐ Requestor
☐ Beneficiary/Derivative   ☐ Respondent (ICE, CBP)

Information About Client (Applicant, Petitioner, Requestor, Beneficiary or Derivative, Respondent, or Authorized Signatory for an Entity)

6.a. Family Name (Last Name) ███████████

6.b. Given Name (First Name) ████████

6.c. Middle Name

7.a. Name of Entity (if applicable)

7.b. Title of Authorized Signatory for Entity (if applicable)

8. Client's USCIS Online Account Number (if any)
  ▶

9. Client's Alien Registration Number (A-Number) (if any)
  ▶ A- ███████████

Client's Contact Information

10. Daytime Telephone Number
  ███████████

11. Mobile Telephone Number (if any)
  ███████████

12. Email Address (if any)

Mailing Address of Client

NOTE: Provide the client's mailing address. **Do not** provide the business mailing address of the attorney or accredited representative **unless** it serves as the safe mailing address on the application or petition being filed with this Form G-28.

13.a. Street Number and Name ███████████

13.b. ☐ Apt. ☐ Ste. ☐ Flr.

13.c. City or Town ███████████

13.d. State **CA**   13.e. ZIP Code ███████████

13.f. Province

13.g. Postal Code

13.h. Country
  USA

Part 4. Client's Consent to Representation and Signature

Consent to Representation and Release of Information

I have requested the representation of and consented to being represented by the attorney or accredited representative named in **Part 1.** of this form. According to the Privacy Act of 1974 and U.S. Department of Homeland Security (DHS) policy, I also consent to the disclosure to the named attorney or accredited representative of any records pertaining to me that appear in any system of records of USCIS, ICE, or CBP.

Part 4. Client's Consent to Representation and Signature (continued)

Options Regarding Receipt of USCIS Notices and Documents

USCIS will send notices to both a represented party (the client) and his, her, or its attorney or accredited representative either through mail or electronic delivery. USCIS will send all secure identity documents and Travel Documents to the client's U.S. mailing address.

If you want to have notices and/or secure identity documents sent to your attorney or accredited representative of record rather than to you, please select all applicable items below. You may change these elections through written notice to USCIS.

1.a. [X] I request that USCIS send original notices on an application or petition to the U.S. business address of my attorney or accredited representative as listed in this form.

1.b. ☐ I request that USCIS send any secure identity document (Permanent Resident Card, Employment Authorization Document, or Travel Document) that I receive to the U.S. business address of my attorney or accredited representative (or to a designated military or diplomatic address in a foreign country (if permitted)).

  NOTE: If your notice contains Form I-94, Arrival-Departure Record, USCIS will send the notice to the U.S. business address of your attorney or accredited representative. If you would rather have your Form I-94 sent directly to you, select **Item Number 1.c.**

1.c. ☐ I request that USCIS send my notice containing Form I-94 to me at my U.S. mailing address

Signature of Client or Authorized Signatory for an Entity

2.a. Signature of Client or Authorized Signatory for an Entity
➡ [signature redacted]

2.b. Date of Signature (mm/dd/yyyy) [redacted]

Part 5. Signature of Attorney or Accredited Representative

I have read and understand the regulations and conditions contained in 8 CFR 103.2 and 292 governing appearances and representation before DHS. I declare under penalty of perjury under the laws of the United States that the information I have provided on this form is true and correct.

1.b. Date of Signature (mm/dd/yyyy) [handwritten]

2.a. Signature of Law Student or Law Graduate

2.b. Date of Signature (mm/dd/yyyy)

Part 6. Additional Information

If you need extra space to provide any additional information within this form, use the space below. If you need more space than what is provided, you may make copies of this page to complete and file with this or attach a separate sheet of paper. Type or print your name at the top of each sheet; indicate the **Page Number**, **Part Number**, and **Item Number** to which your answer refers; and sign and date each sheet.

1.a Family Name
(Last Name) ███████████ █████████

1.b. Given Name
(First Name) ███████

1.c. Middle Name

2.a. Page Number   2.b. Part Number   2.c. Item Number

2.d.

4.a. Page Number   4.b. Part Number   4.c. Item Number

4.d.

5.a. Page Number   5.b. Part Number   5.c. Item Number

5.d.

3.a. Page Number   3.b. Part Number   3.c. Item Number

3.d.

6.a. Page Number   6.b. Part Number   6.c. Item Number

6.d.

Pg 8

Petition for Alien Relative

Department of Homeland Security
U.S. Citizenship and Immigration Services

USCIS
Form I-130
OMB No. 1615-0012
Expires 07/31/2018

For USCIS Use Only		
A-Number	Fee Stamp	Action Stamp

A-

Initial Receipt	
Resubmitted	

Relocated	Section of Law/Visa Category		
Received	☐ 201(b) Spouse - IR-1/CR-1	☐ 203(a)(1) Unm. S/D - F1-1	☐ 203(a)(2)(B) Unm. S/D - F2-4
Sent	☐ 201(b) Child - IR-2/CR-2	☐ 203(a)(2)(A) Spouse - F2-1	☐ 203(a)(3) Married S/D - F3-1
Completed	☐ 201(b) Parent - IR-5	☐ 203(a)(2)(A) Child - F2-2	☐ 203(a)(4) Brother/Sister - F4-1

Approved	Petition was filed on (Priority Date mm/dd/yyyy):	☐ Field Investigation	☐ Personal Interview	☐ 204(a)(2)(A) Resolved
		☐ Previously Forwarded	☐ Pet. A-File Reviewed	☐ I-485 Filed Simultaneously
Returned	PDR request granted/denied - New priority date (mm/dd/yyyy):	☐ 203(g) Resolved	☐ Ben. A-File Reviewed	☐ 204(g) Resolved

Remarks	

At which USCIS office (e.g., NBC, VSC, LOS, CRO) was Form I-130 adjudicated? _____

To be completed by an attorney or accredited representative (if any).			
☒ Select this box if Form G-28 is attached.	**Volag Number** (if any)	**Attorney State Bar Number** (if applicable) ▮▮▮	**Attorney or Accredited Representative USCIS Online Account Number** (if any)

▶ **START HERE - Type or print in black ink.**

If you need extra space to complete any section of this petition, use the space provided in Part 9. Additional Information. Complete and submit as many copies of Part 9., as necessary, with your petition.

Part 1. Relationship (You are the Petitioner. Your relative is the Beneficiary)

1. I am filing this petition for my (Select only one box):

   ☐ Spouse ☐ Parent ☐ Brother/Sister ☒ Child

2. If you are filing this petition for your child or parent, select the box that describes your relationship (Select only one box):

   ☐ Child was born to parents who were married to each other at the time of the child's birth

   ☐ Stepchild/Stepparent

   ☐ Child was born to parents who were not married to each other at the time of the child's birth

   ☐ Child was adopted (not an Orphan or Hague Convention adoptee)

3. If the beneficiary is your brother/sister, are you related by adoption? ☐ Yes ☒ No

4. Did you gain lawful permanent resident status or citizenship through adoption? ☐ Yes ☒ No

Part 2. Information About You (Petitioner)

1. Alien Registration Number (A-Number) (if any)

   ▶ A- ▮▮▮▮▮▮▮▮

2. USCIS Online Account Number (if any)

   ▶

3. U.S. Social Security Number (if any)

   ▶ ▮▮▮▮

Your Full Name

4.a. Family Name (Last Name) ▮▮▮

4.b. Given Name (First Name) ▮▮▮

4.c. Middle Name

Part 2. Information About You (Petitioner) (continued)

Other Names Used (if any)

Provide all other names you have ever used, including aliases, maiden name, and nicknames.

5.a.	Family Name (Last Name)	None
5.b.	Given Name (First Name)	
5.c.	Middle Name	

Other Information

6. City/Town/Village of Birth

███████████████

7. Country of Birth

███████

8. Date of Birth (mm/dd/yyyy) **01/19/1965**

9. Sex ☒ Male ☐ Female

Mailing Address

10.a. In Care Of Name

███████████████

10.b. Street Number and Name ███████████████

10.c. ☐ Apt. ☐ Ste. ☐ Flr.

10.d. City or Town ███████████

10.e. State **CA** 10.f. ZIP Code ███████

10.g. Province

10.h. Postal Code

10.i. Country

USA

11. Is your current mailing address the same as your physical address? ☒ Yes ☐ No

If you answered "No" to Item Number 11., provide information on your physical address in Item Numbers 12.a. - 13.b.

Address History

Provide your physical addresses for the last five years, whether inside or outside the United States. Provide your current address first if it is different from your mailing address in Item Numbers 10.a. - 10.i.

Physical Address 1

12.a. Street Number and Name

12.b. ☐ Apt. ☐ Ste. ☐ Flr.

12.c. City or Town

12.d. State 12.e. ZIP Code

12.f. Province

12.g. Postal Code

12.h. Country

13.a. Date From (mm/dd/yyyy)

13.b. Date To (mm/dd/yyyy) **PRESENT**

Physical Address 2

14.a. Street Number and Name ███████ ███████████

14.b. ☐ Apt. ☐ Ste. ☐ Flr.

14.c. City or Town ██████████

14.d. State **CA** 14.e. ZIP Code ██████

14.f. Province

14.g. Postal Code

14.h. Country

USA

15.a. Date From (mm/dd/yyyy) **01/01/2012**

15.b. Date To (mm/dd/yyyy) **11/01/2016**

Your Marital Information

16. How many times have you been married? ► **1**

17. Current Marital Status

☐ Single, Never Married ☒ Married ☐ Divorced
☐ Widowed ☐ Separated ☐ Annulled

Pg 10

Part 2. Information About You (Petitioner) (continued)

18. Date of Current Marriage (if currently married) (mm/dd/yyyy) **01/10/1996**

Place of Your Current Marriage (if married)

19.a. City or Town ███████████████

19.b. State ☐

19.c. Province ███ ██ ████

19.d. Country ████

Names of All Your Spouses (if any)

Provide information on your current spouse (if currently married) first and then list all your prior spouses (if any).

Spouse 1

20.a. Family Name (Last Name) ███████████

20.b. Given Name (First Name) ███

20.c. Middle Name ███████████████

21. Date Marriage Ended (mm/dd/yyyy)

Spouse 2

22.a. Family Name (Last Name)

22.b. Given Name (First Name)

22.c. Middle Name

23. Date Marriage Ended (mm/dd/yyyy)

Information About Your Parents

Parent 1's Information

Full Name of Parent 1

24.a. Family Name (Last Name) ███████████

24.b. Given Name (First Name) ██████

24.c. Middle Name

25. Date of Birth (mm/dd/yyyy) **01/18/1946**

26. Sex ☒ Male ☐ Female

27. Country of Birth ████

28. City/Town/Village of Residence ████

29. Country of Residence ████

Parent 2's Information

Full Name of Parent 2

30.a. Family Name (Last Name) ████████████

30.b. Given Name (First Name) ███

30.c. Middle Name

31. Date of Birth (mm/dd/yyyy) **10/27/1948**

32. Sex ☐ Male ☒ Female

33. Country of Birth **Mexico**

34. C___n/Village of Residence ████

35. Country of Residence **Mexico**

Additional Information About You (Petitioner)

36. I am a (Select only one box):
    ☐ U.S. Citizen ☒ Lawful Permanent Resident

If you are a U.S. citizen, complete Item Number 37.

37. My citizenship was acquired through (Select only one box):
    ☐ Birth in the United States
    ☐ Naturalization
    ☐ Parents

38. Have you obtained a Certificate of Naturalization or a Certificate of Citizenship? ☐ Yes ☐ No

If you answered "Yes" to Item Number 38., complete the following:

39.a. Certificate Number

39.b. Place of Issuance

39.c. Date of Issuance (mm/dd/yyyy)

Pg 11

Part 2. Information About You (Petitioner) (continued)

If you are a lawful permanent resident, complete Item Numbers 40.a. - 41.

40.a. Class of Admission

S26

40.b. Date of Admission (mm/dd/yyyy)   12/01/1990

Place of Admission

40.c. City or Town

Los Angeles

40.d State   CA

41. Did you gain lawful permanent resident status through marriage to a U.S. citizen or lawful permanent resident?

☐ Yes   ☒ No

Employment History

Provide your employment history for the last five years, whether inside or outside the United States. Provide your current employment first. If you are currently unemployed, type or print "Unemployed" in Item Number 42.

Employer 1

42. Name of Employer/Company

▮▮▮▮▮▮▮▮

43.a. Street Number and Name   ▮▮▮▮ . ▮▮▮▮

43.b. ☐ Apt. ☒ Ste. ☐ Flr.   110

43.c. City or Town   ▮▮▮▮

43.d. State   CA   43.e. ZIP Code   ▮▮▮

43.f. Province

43.g. Postal Code

43.h. Country

USA

44. Your Occupation

Horse Groomer

45.a. Date From (mm/dd/yyyy)   11/01/2016

45.b. Date To (mm/dd/yyyy)   PRESENT

Employer 2

46. Name of Employer/Company

▮▮▮▮▮▮▮▮

47.a. Street Number and Name   ▮▮▮ ▮▮▮▮

47.b. ☐ Apt. ☐ Ste. ☐ Flr.

47.c. City or Town   ▮▮▮

47.d. State   CA   47.e. ZIP Code   91 066

47.f. Province

47.g. Postal Code

47.h. Country

USA

48. Your Occupation

Horse Groomer

49.a. Date From (mm/dd/yyyy)   05/01/2016

49.b. Date To (mm/dd/yyyy)   11/01/2016

Part 3. Biographic Information

NOTE: Provide the biographic information about you, the petitioner.

1. Ethnicity (Select only one box)

   [X] Hispanic or Latino
   ☐ Not Hispanic or Latino

2. Race (Select all applicable boxes)

   ☒ White
   ☐ Asian
   ☐ Black or African American
   ☐ American Indian or Alaska Native
   ☐ Native Hawaiian or Other Pacific Islander

3. Height   Feet | 5 | Inches | 5 |

4. Weight   Pounds | 1 | 3 | 0 |

5. Eye Color (Select only one box)

   ☐ Black   ☐ Blue   ☒ Brown
   ☐ Gray   ☐ Green   ☐ Hazel
   ☐ Maroon   ☐ Pink   ☐ Unknown/Other

Part 3. Biographic Information (continued)

6. Hair Color (Select only one box)

- [ ] Bald (No hair)
- [ ] Black
- [ ] Blond
- [X] Brown
- [ ] Gray
- [ ] Red
- [ ] Sandy
- [ ] White
- [ ] Unknown/Other

Part 4. Information About Beneficiary

1. Alien Registration Number (A-Number) (if any)

▶ A- _____

2. USCIS Online Account Number (if any)

▶ _____

3. U.S. Social Security Number (if any)

▶ _____

Beneficiary's Full Name

4.a. Family Name (Last Name) _____

4.b. Given Name (First Name) _____ ld

4.c. Middle Name _____

Other Names Used (if any)

Provide all other names the beneficiary has ever used, including aliases, maiden name, and nicknames.

5.a. Family Name (Last Name) **None**

5.b. Given Name (First Name) _____

5.c. Middle Name _____

Other Information About Beneficiary

6. City/Town/Village of Birth

_____

7. Country of Birth

_____

8. Date of Birth (mm/dd/yyyy) **11/06/2001**

9. Sex [ ] Male [X] Female

10. Has anyone else ever filed a petition for the beneficiary?

[ ] Yes [X] No [ ] Unknown

NOTE: Select "Unknown" *only* if you do not know, and the beneficiary also does not know, if anyone else has ever filed a petition for the beneficiary.

Beneficiary's Physical Address

If the beneficiary lives outside the United States in a home without a street number or name, leave Item Numbers 11.a. and 11.b. blank.

11.a _____

11.b. [ ] Apt. [ ] Ste. [ ] Flr. _____

11.c. City or Town _____

11.d. State _____ 11.e. ZIP Code _____

11.f. Province _____

11.g. Postal Code **43500**

11.h. Country

Mexico

Other Address and Contact Information

Provide the address in the United States where the beneficiary intends to live, if different from Item Numbers 11.a. - 11.h. If the address is the same, type or print "SAME" in Item Number 12.a.

12.a Street Number and Name _____

12.b. [ ] Apt. [ ] Ste. [ ] Flr. _____

12.c. City or Town _____

12.d. State **CA** 12.e. ZIP Code **90720**

Provide the beneficiary's address outside the United States, if different from Item Numbers 11.a. - 11.h. If the address is the same, type or print "SAME" in Item Number 13.a.

13.a. Street Number and Name _____

13.b. [ ] Apt. [ ] Ste. [ ] Flr. _____

13.c. City or Town _____

13.d. Province _____

13.e. Postal Code _____

13.f. Country

_____

14. Daytime Telephone Number (if any)

_____

Part 4. Information About Beneficiary (continued)

15. Mobile Telephone Number (if any)

▮▮▮▮▮▮▮▮▮▮▮▮▮▮

16. Email Address (if any)

▮▮▮▮▮▮▮▮▮▮▮▮▮▮▮▮▮▮

Beneficiary's Marital Information

17. How many times has the beneficiary been married?

▶ 0

18. Current Marital Status

☒ Single, Never Married ☐ Married ☐ Divorced

☐ Widowed ☐ Separated ☐ Annulled

19. Date of Current Marriage (if currently married) (mm/dd/yyyy)

Place of Beneficiary's Current Marriage (if married)

20.a. City or Town

20.b. State

20.c. Province

20.d. Country

Names of Beneficiary's Spouses (if any)

Provide information on the beneficiary's current spouse (if currently married) first and then list all the beneficiary's prior spouses (if any).

Spouse 1

21.a. Family Name (Last Name) **None**

21.b. Given Name (First Name)

21.c. Middle Name

22. Date Marriage Ended (mm/dd/yyyy)

Spouse 2

23.a. Family Name (Last Name)

23.b. Given Name (First Name)

23.c. Middle Name

24. Date Marriage Ended (mm/dd/yyyy)

Information About Beneficiary's Family

Provide information about the beneficiary's spouse and children.

Person 1

25.a. Family Name (Last Name)

25.b. Given Name (First Name)

25.c. Middle Name

26. Relationship

27. Date of Birth (mm/dd/yyyy)

28. Country of Birth

Person 2

29.a. Family Name (Last Name)

29.b. Given Name (First Name)

29.c. Middle Name

30. Relationship

31. Date of Birth (mm/dd/yyyy)

32. Country of Birth

Person 3

33.a. Family Name (Last Name)

33.b. Given Name (First Name)

33.c. Middle Name

34. Relationship

35. Date of Birth (mm/dd/yyyy)

36. Country of Birth

Pg 14

Part 4. Information About Beneficiary (continued)

Person 4

37.a. Family Name
(Last Name)

37.b. Given Name
(First Name)

37.c. Middle Name

38. Relationship

39. Date of Birth (mm/dd/yyyy)

40. Country of Birth

Person 5

41.a. Family Name
(Last Name)

41.b. Given Name
(First Name)

41.c. Middle Name

42. Relationship

43. Date of Birth (mm/dd/yyyy)

44. Country of Birth

Beneficiary's Entry Information

45. Was the beneficiary EVER in the United States?

☐ Yes ☒ No

If the beneficiary is currently in the United States, complete **Items Numbers 46.a. - 46.d.**

46.a. He or she arrived as a (Class of Admission):

46.b. Form I-94 Arrival-Departure Record Number

▶

46.c. Date of Arrival (mm/dd/yyyy)

46.d. Date authorized stay expired, or will expire, as shown on Form I-94 or Form I-95 (mm/dd/yyyy) or type or print "D/S" for Duration of Status

47. Passport Number

████████

48. Travel Document Number

49. Country of Issuance for Passport or Travel Document

Mexico

50. Expiration Date for Passport or Travel Document (mm/dd/yyyy)

08/31/2021

Beneficiary's Employment Information

Provide the beneficiary's current employment information (if applicable), even if they are employed outside of the United States. If the beneficiary is currently unemployed, type or print "Unemployed" in **Item Number 51.a.**

51.a. Name of Current Employer (if applicable)

Unemployed

51.b. Street Number
and Name

51.c. ☐ Apt. ☐ Ste. ☐ Flr.

51.d. City or Town

51.e. State   51.f. ZIP Code

51.g. Province

51.h. Postal Code

51.i. Country

52. Date Employment Began (mm/dd/yyyy)

Additional Information About Beneficiary

53. Was the beneficiary EVER in immigration proceedings?

☐ Yes ☒ No

54. If you answered "Yes," select the type of proceedings and provide the location and date of the proceedings.

☐ Removal   ☐ Exclusion/Deportation

☐ Rescission   ☐ Other Judicial Proceedings

55.a. City or Town

55.b. State

56. Date (mm/dd/yyyy)

Pg 15

Part 4. Information About Beneficiary (continued)

If the beneficiary's native written language does not use Roman letters, type or print his or her name and foreign address in their native written language.

57.a. Family Name (Last Name) [ ]

57.b. Given Name (First Name) [ ]

57.c. Middle Name [ ]

58.a. Street Number and Name [ ]

58.b. ☐ Apt. ☐ Ste. ☐ Flr. [ ]

58.c. City or Town [ ]

58.d. Province [ ]

58.e. Postal Code [ ]

58.f. Country [ ]

If filing for your spouse, provide the last address at which you physically lived together. If you never lived together, type or print, "Never lived together" in Item Number 59.a.

59.a. Street Number and Name [ ]

59.b. ☐ Apt. ☐ Ste. ☐ Flr. [ ]

59.c. City or Town [ ]

59.d. State [ ]   59.e. ZIP Code [ ]

59.f. Province [ ]

59.g. Postal Code [ ]

59.h. Country [ ]

60.a. Date From (mm/dd/yyyy) [ ]

60.b. Date To (mm/dd/yyyy) [ ]

The beneficiary is in the United States and will apply for adjustment of status to that of a lawful permanent resident at the U.S. Citizenship and Immigration Services (USCIS) office in:

61.a. City or Town [ ]

61.b. State [ ]

The beneficiary will not apply for adjustment of status in the United States, but he or she will apply for an immigrant visa abroad at the U.S. Embassy or U.S. Consulate in:

62.a. City or Town [▮▮▮▮]

62.b. Province [▮▮▮]

62.c. Country

Mexico

NOTE: Choosing a U.S. Embassy or U.S. Consulate outside the country of the beneficiary's last residence does not guarantee that it will accept the beneficiary's case for processing. In these situations, the designated U.S. Embassy or U.S. Consulate has discretion over whether or not to accept the beneficiary's case.

Part 5. Other Information

1. Have you EVER previously filed a petition for this beneficiary or any other alien?   ☒ Yes ☐ No

If you answered "Yes," provide the name, place, date of filing, and the result.

2.a. Family Name (Last Name) [▮▮▮▮▮▮]

2.b. Given Name (First Name) [▮▮▮]

2.c. Middle Name [▮▮▮]

3.a. City or Town Los Angeles

3.b. State CA

4. Date Filed (mm/dd/yyyy) 10/01/2018

5. Result (for example, approved, denied, withdrawn)

Pending

If you are also submitting separate petitions for other relatives, provide the names of and your relationship to each relative

Relative 1

6.a. Family Name (Last Name) [▮▮▮▮▮]

6.b. Given Name (First Name) [▮▮]

6.c. Middle Name [▮▮▮]

7. Relationship [▮▮]

Pg 16

Part 5. Other Information (continued)

Relative 2

8.a.	Family Name (Last Name)	████████████
8.b.	Given Name (First Name)	████
8.c.	Middle Name	
9.	Relationship	Daughter

WARNING: USCIS investigates the claimed relationships and verifies the validity of documents you submit. If you falsify a family relationship to obtain a visa, USCIS may seek to have you criminally prosecuted.

PENALTIES: By law, you may be imprisoned for up to 5 years or fined $250,000, or both, for entering into a marriage contract in order to evade any U.S. immigration law. In addition, you may be fined up to $10,000 and imprisoned for up to 5 years, or both, for knowingly and willfully falsifying or concealing a material fact or using any false document in submitting this petition.

Part 6. Petitioner's Statement, Contact Information, Declaration, and Signature

NOTE: Read the **Penalties** section of the Form I-130 Instructions before completing this part.

Petitioner's Statement

NOTE: Select the box for either **Item Number 1.a.** or **1.b.** If applicable, select the box for **Item Number 2.**

1.a. ☐ I can read and understand English, and I have read and understand every question and instruction on this petition and my answer to every question.

1.b. ☒ The interpreter named in **Part 7.** read to me every question and instruction on this petition and my answer to every question in

Spanish

a language in which I am fluent. I understood all of this information as interpreted.

2. ☒ At my request, the preparer named in **Part 8.**,

████████████

prepared thi██████████ based only upon information I provided or authorized.

Petitioner's Contact Information

3. Petitioner's Daytime Telephone Number

████████████

4. Petitioner's Mobile Telephone Number (if any)

████████████

5. Petitioner's Email Address (if any)

Petitioner's Declaration and Certification

Copies of any documents I have submitted are exact photocopies of unaltered, original documents, and I understand that USCIS may require that I submit original documents to USCIS at a later date. Furthermore, I authorize the release of any information from any of my records that USCIS may need to determine my eligibility for the immigration benefit I seek.

I further authorize release of information contained in this petition, in supporting documents, and in my USCIS records to other entities and persons where necessary for the administration and enforcement of U.S. immigration laws.

I understand that USCIS may require me to appear for an appointment to take my biometrics (fingerprints, photograph, and/or signature) and, at that time, if I am required to provide biometrics, I will be required to sign an oath reaffirming that:

1) I provided or authorized all of the information contained in, and submitted with, my petition;

2) I reviewed and understood all of the information in, and submitted with, my petition; and

3) All of this information was complete, true, and correct at the time of filing.

I certify, under penalty of perjury, that all of the information in my petition and any document submitted with it were provided or authorized by me, that I reviewed and understand all of the information contained in, and submitted with, my petition, and that all of this information is complete, true, and correct.

Petitioner's Signature

6.a. Petitioner's Signature (sign in ink)

➡ ████████████

6.b. Date of Signature (mm/dd/yyyy)   10/22/2018

NOTE TO ALL PETITIONERS: If you do not completely fill out this petition or fail to submit required documents listed in the Instructions, USCIS may deny your petition.

Part 7. Interpreter's Contact Information, Certification, and Signature

Provide the following information about the interpreter if you used one.

Interpreter's Full Name

1.a. Interpreter's Family Name (Last Name)

▮▮▮▮▮

1.b. In ▮▮▮ ven Name (First Name)

▮▮▮▮▮

2. In ▮▮▮ ter's Business or Organization Name (if any)

Law Offices of Brian D. Lerner, APC

Interpreter's Mailing Address

3.a. Street Number and Name | 3233 E. Broadway

3.b. ☐ Apt. ☐ Ste. ☐ Flr.

3.c. City or Town | Long Beach

3.d. State | CA   3.e. ZIP Code | 90803

3.f. Province

3.g. Postal Code

3.h. Country

USA

Interpreter's Contact Information

4. Interpreter's Daytime Telephone Number

▮▮▮▮▮

5. In ▮▮▮ Telephone Number (if any)

6. Interpreter's Email Address (if any)

▮▮▮▮▮

Interpreter's Certification

I certify, under penalty of perjury, that:

I am fluent in English and | Spanish

which is the same language provided in Part 6., Item Number 1.b., and I have read to this petitioner in the identified language every question and instruction on this petition and his or her answer to every question. The petitioner informed me that he or she understands every instruction, question, and answer on the petition, including the **Petitioner's Declaration and Certification**, and has verified the accuracy of every answer.

Interpreter's Signature

7.a. Interpreter's Signature (sign in ink)

7.b. Date of Signature (mm/dd/yyyy) | 1C 22 / 18

Part 8. Contact Information, Declaration, and Signature of the Person Preparing this Petition, if Other Than the Petitioner

Provide the following information about the preparer.

Preparer's Full Name

1.a. Preparer's Family Name (Last Name)

▮▮▮▮▮

1.b. Preparer's Given Name (First Name)

▮▮▮▮▮

2. ▮▮▮ ss or Organization Name (if any)

Law Offices of Brian D. Lerner, APC

Preparer's Mailing Address

3.a. Street Number and Name | 3233 E. Broadway

3.b. ☐ Apt. ☐ Ste. ☐ Flr.

3.c. City or Town | Long Beach

3.d. State | CA   3.e. ZIP Code | 90803

3.f. Province

3.g. Postal Code

3.h. Country

USA

Part 8. Contact Information, Declaration, and
Signature of the Person Preparing this Petition, if
Other Than the Petitioner (continued)

Preparer's Contact Information

4. Preparer's Daytime Telephone Number

   (562) 495-0554

5. Preparer's Mobile Telephone Number (if any)

6. Preparer's Email Address (if any)

   ███████████████

Preparer's Statement

7.a. ☐ I am not an attorney or accredited representative but
have prepared this petition on behalf of the petitioner
and with the petitioner's consent.

7.b. ☒ I am an attorney or accredited representative and my
representation of the petitioner in this case
☒ extends ☐ does not extend beyond the preparation
of this petition.

NOTE: If you are an attorney or accredited
representative whose representation extends beyond
preparation of this petition, you may be obliged to
submit a completed Form G-28, Notice of Entry of
Appearance as Attorney or Accredited
Representative, with this petition.

Preparer's Certification

By my signature, I certify, under penalty of perjury, that I
prepared this petition at the request of the petitioner. The
petitioner then reviewed this completed petition and informed
me that he or she understands all of the information contained
in, and submitted with, his or her petition, including the
Petitioner's Declaration and Certification, and that all of this
information is complete, true, and correct. I completed this
petition based only on information that the petitioner provided
to me or authorized me to obtain or use.

Preparer's Signature

8.a. Preparer's Signature (sign in ink)

   ████████████████████████

8.b. Date of Signature (mm/dd/yyyy)   10/22/15

Part 9. Additional Information

If you need extra space to provide any additional information within this petition, use the space below. If you need more space than what is provided, you may make copies of this page to complete and file with this petition or attach a separate sheet of paper. Type or print your name and A-Number (if any) at the top of each sheet; indicate the **Page Number, Part Number,** and **Item Number** to which your answer refers; and sign and date each sheet.

1.a. Family Name (Last Name) ████████ ████████

1.b. Given Name (First Name) ████

1.c. Middle Name

2. A-Number (if any) ▶ A- ██ █ █ ██ █ █ ██

3.a. Page Number

3.b. Part Number

3.c. Item Number

3.d.

4.a. Page Number

4.b. Part Number

4.c. Item Number

4.d.

5.a. Page Number

5.b. Part Number

5.c. Item Number

5.d.

6.a. Page Number

6.b. Part Number

6.c. Item Number

6.d.

7.a. Page Number

7.b. Part Number

7.c. Item Number

7.d.

Pg 20

Addendum

████████████████ ████████ Form: I-130 (Page 1)

Part 2.: Additional Employment History of Petitioner:

Employer: ████████████ ████████████████████

Type of Work: Horse Groomer
Period: 01/01/2015 - 05/01/2016
Employer: ████████ ████████████████████████████████

Type of Work: Horse Groomer
Period: 01/01/2012 - 01/01/2015

SECTION 3:

Exhibits

Exhibit '1'

Copy of Petitioner's Birth Certificate with English Translation

*** English Extract of Spanish Birth Certificate***
Civil Registration

Name of Registered Child: ███████████████████

    Sex: Male

    Date of Birth: 01/19/1965

    Place of Birth: Jaltepec, Tulancingo, Hidalgo, Mexico

Father of Child: ████████████████

    Nationality: Mexican

    Age: ------- yrs.

Mother of Child: ████████████████

    Nationality: Mexican

    Age   ------- yrs.

Certificate Information

Registration Date:	02/17/1965
Place of Issue:	Acatlan, Hidalgo, Mexico
Magistrate:	Alfredo Arciniega Olvera
Record Location:	Acatlan, Hidalgo, Mexico
Certificate:	No. 00080
Folio:	No. 21
Book:	No. 01

Translator's Certificate of Competence

I, ████████████████, certify that the above is an accurate translation of the original Birth Certificate in Spanish and that I am competent in both English and Spanish to render such translation.

████████████████████   ████████████████

                                                     Date

Law Offices of Brian D. Lerner
3233 East Broadway
Long Beach, CA 90803
Tel: (562) 495-0554

Estado Libre y Soberano
de Hidalgo

EN NOMBRE DEL ESTADO LIBRE Y SOBERANO DE HIDALGO Y COMO OFICIAL DEL REGISTRO DEL ESTADO FAMILIAR, HAGO SABER
A LOS QUE LA PRESENTE VIEREN, Y CERTIFICO QUE EN EL LIBRO NUMERO ___01___ DEL REGISTRO QUE ES A MI CARGO, A LA FOJA ___21___
SE ENCUENTRAN ASENTADOS LOS DATOS SIGUIENTES:

ACTA DE NACIMIENTO

CRIP: ----------
CURP: ----------

OFICIALIA	LIBRO No.	ACTA No.	LOCALIDAD		FECHA DE REGISTRO
01	01	00080	ACATLAN		DIA MES AÑO 17/FEBRERO/1965

MUNICIPIO O DELEGACION	ENTIDAD FEDERATIVA
ACATLAN	HIDALGO

DATOS DEL REGISTRADO

▇▇▇	CERVANTES	▇▇▇
NOMBRE(S)	PRIMER APELLIDO	SEGUNDO APELLIDO
MEXICANA	MASCULINO	
NACIONALIDAD	SEXO	

LUGAR Y FECHA DE NACIMIENTO

LOCALIDAD	MUNICIPIO	ENTIDAD	PAIS	FECHA
JALTEPEC	TULANCINGO	HIDALGO	MEXICO	19/ENERO/1965

COMPARECIO: EL PADRE

DATOS DE LOS PADRES

LEOBARDO	CERVANTES	----------
NOMBRE(S)	PRIMER APELLIDO	SEGUNDO APELLIDO
MEXICANA		
NACIONALIDAD		
OFELIA	▇▇▇	----------
NOMBRE(S)	PRIMER APELLIDO	SEGUNDO APELLIDO
MEXICANA		
NACIONALIDAD		

DATOS DE LOS ABUELOS

ABUELO PATERNO: ----------	NACIONALIDAD: ----------
ABUELA PATERNA: ----------	NACIONALIDAD: ----------
ABUELO MATERNO: ----------	NACIONALIDAD: ----------
ABUELA MATERNA: ----------	NACIONALIDAD: ----------

LA PRESENTE ACTA CONTIENE ANOTACIONES AL REVERSO:

SE EXTIENDE ESTA CERTIFICACION EN CUMPLIMIENTO DEL ARTICULO 406 DE LA LEY PARA LA FAMILIA VIGENTE EN EL ESTADO
DE HIDALGO, EN ACATLAN, HGO. EL SUSCRITO OFICIAL DEL REGISTRO DEL ESTADO FAMILIAR

LIC. ALFREDO ARCINIEGA OLVERA

27/03/2013 13:27:25

2012 - 2016
SELLO DE LA OFICIALIA
DEL REGISTRO DEL
ESTADO FAMILIAR
43.38....

Exhibit '2'

Copy of Petitioner's Legal Permanent Residence

Pg 27

Exhibit '3'

Copy of Beneficiary's Birth Certificate with English Translation

*** English Extract of Spanish Birth Certificate***
Civil Registration

Name of Registered Child: ██████████████████████████

    Sex: Female

    Date of Birth: 11/06/2001

    Place of Birth: Tulancingo, Hidalgo, Mexico

Father of Child: ██████████████████████████

    Nationality: Mexican

    Age: ------- yrs.

Mother of Child: ██████████████ ██████████

    Nationality: Mexican

    Age   -------- yrs.

Certificate Information

Registration Date:	02/18/2002
Place of Issue:	Huasca de Ocampo, Hidalgo, Mexico
Magistrate:	C. Margarita Sosa-Gutierrez
Record Location:	Huasca de Ocampo, Hidalgo, Mexico
Certificate:	No. 00055
Folio:	No. 5352786
Book:	No. 01

Translator's Certificate of Competence

I, ██████████████, certify that the above is an accurate translation of the original Birth Certificate in Spanish and that I am competent in both English and Spanish to render such translation.

██████████████████████████

_10/22/18_
Date

Law Offices of Brian D. Lerner
3233 East Broadway
Long Beach, CA 90803
Tel: (562) 495-0554

Pg 29

Estado Libre y Soberano
de Hidalgo

EN NOMBRE DEL ESTADO LIBRE Y SOBERANO DE HIDALGO Y COMO OFICIAL DEL REGISTRO DEL ESTADO FAMILIAR, HAGO SABER A LOS QUE LA PRESENTE VIEREN, Y CERTIFICO QUE EN EL LIBRO NUMERO   01   DEL REGISTRO QUE ES A MI CARGO, A LA FOJA   55
SE ENCUENTRAN ASENTADOS LOS DATOS SIGUIENTES

ACTA DE NACIMIENTO

CRIP	13024010200055E
CURP	

OFICIALIA	LIBRO No	ACTA No	LOCALIDAD	FECHA DE REGISTRO
01	01	00055	HUASCA DE OCAMPO	DIA MES AÑO 18/FEBRERO/2002

MUNICIPIO O DELEGACION	ENTIDAD FEDERATIVA
HUASCA DE OCAMPO	HIDALGO

DATOS DEL REGISTRADO

▇▇▇	CERVANTES	BARRON
NOMBRE(S)	PRIMER APELLIDO	SEGUNDO APELLIDO
MEXICANA	FEMENINO	
NACIONALIDAD	SEXO	

LUGAR Y FECHA DE NACIMIENTO

LOCALIDAD	MUNICIPIO	ENTIDAD	PAIS	FECHA
TULANCINGO	TULANCINGO	HIDALGO	MEXICO	06/NOVIEMBRE/2001

COMPARECIO: AMBOS

DATOS DE LOS PADRES

MARTIN	CERVANTES	▇▇▇
NOMBRE(S)	PRIMER APELLIDO	SEGUNDO APELLIDO
MEXICANA		
NACIONALIDAD		
MARIA GUADALUPE	▇▇▇	PEREZ
NOMBRE(S)	PRIMER APELLIDO	SEGUNDO APELLIDO
MEXICANA		
NACIONALIDAD		

DATOS DE LOS ABUELOS

ABUELO PATERNO: LEOBARDO CERVANTES SANCHEZ (FINADO)   NACIONALIDAD: MEXICANA

ABUELA PATERNA: OFELIA ▇▇▇ FLORES   NACIONALIDAD MEXICANA

ABUELO MATERNO SANTIAGO ▇▇▇ CANO (FINADO)   NACIONALIDAD MEXICANA

ABUELA MATERNA ANTONIA PEREZ DIMAS   NACIONALIDAD: MEXICANA

SE EXTIENDE ESTA CERTIFICACION EN CUMPLIMIENTO DEL ARTICULO 405 DE LA LEY PARA LA FAMILIA VIGENTE EN EL ESTADO
DE HIDALGO, EN HUASCA DE OCAMPO, HGO. EL SUSCRITO OFICIAL DEL REGISTRO DEL ESTADO FAMILIAR

C. MARGARITA SOSA GUTIERREZ

28/11/2014 10:44:46

5352786

Pg 30

Exhibit '4'

Copy of Beneficiary's Foreign Passport

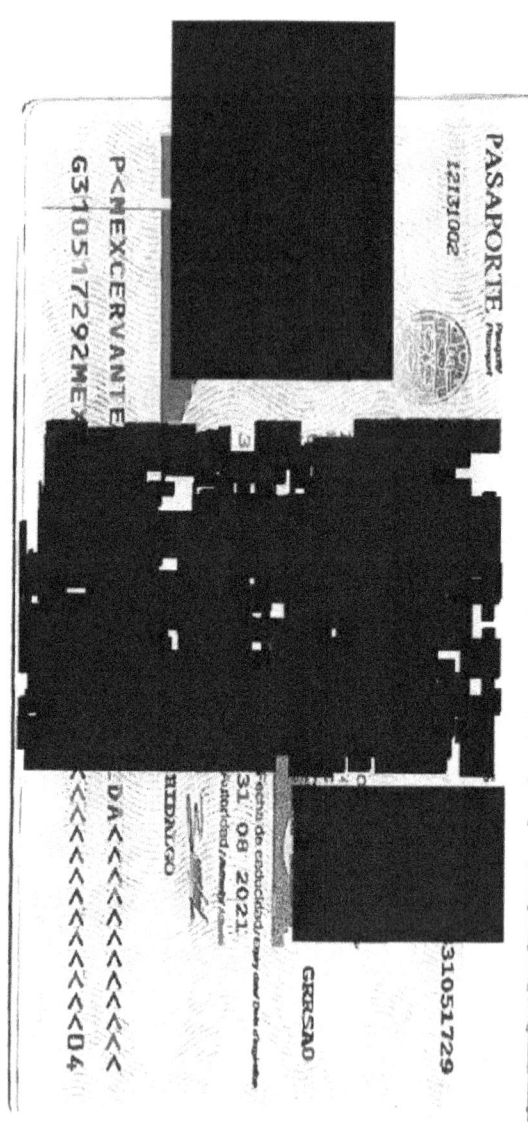

G310517292

PASAPORTE

12131002

P<MEXCERVANTE

G310517292MEX

<<<<<<<<<<
<<<<<<<<<
<<<<<<<<
<<<<<<<<<
<<<<<<<<<
<<<<<<<<<
<<<<<<04

DA<<<<<<<<

HIDALGO

31 08 2021

Fecha de expedición. Expiry and Date d'expiration
Autoridad / Authority / Autorité

GRRESAD

31051729

G310517292

En caso de que el titular de este pasaporte requiera de asistencia o protección del gobierno mexicano, se recomienda que acuda a la representación diplomática o consular mexicana más cercana.

Baja California

Nombre:_____

Dirección:_____

Entidad Federativa:_____

C.P._____ Teléfono:_____

Dirección:_____

Entidad Federativa:_____

C.P._____ Teléfono:_____

Exhibit '5'

Copy of Petitioner's Marriage Certificate

*** English Extract of Spanish Marriage Certificate***
Civil Registration

Groom's Name: ███████████████████ (Sex: Male)
Age: 30 years
Birth Place: Jaltepec, Tulancingo, Hidalgo
Nationality: Mexican
Father's Name: ███████████████
Nationality: Mexican
Mother's Name: ███ ██████████
Nationality: Mexican

Bride's Name: ██████████ ██████████ (Sex: Female)
Age: 18 years
Birth Place: Tulpetlac, Mexico City
Nationality: Mexican
Father's Name: █████ █████████
Nationality: Mexican
Mother's Name: ███████████
Nationality: Mexican

Certificate Information

Issue Date: 01/10/1996
Place of Issue: Atotonilco El Grande, Hidalgo, Mexico
Magistrate: Yolanda Chapa-Carreon
Record Location: Book No. 1 / Certificate No. 04
Folio No.:   04

Translator's Certificate of Competence

I ████████████ certify that the above is an accurate translation of the original Marriage Certificate in Spanish and that I am competent in both English and Spanish to render such translation.

████████████████████

9/27/18
Date

Law Offices of Brian D. Lerner
3233 E. Broadway Avenue Long Beach, CA 90803

Pg 34

ESTADOS UNIDOS MEXICANOS
ESTADO LIBRE Y SOBERANO DE HIDALGO
REGISTRO DEL ESTADO FAMILIAR

No. DE CONTROL

145

EN NOMBRE DEL ESTADO LIBRE Y SOBERANO DE HIDALGO, Y COMO OFICIAL DEL REGISTRO DEL ESTADO FAMILIAR DE ESTE MUNICIPIO, C E R T I F I C O :

SER CIERTO QUE EN EL LIBRO NUM. _____ UNO _____ DEL AÑO _____ 1996 _____ DEL REGISTRO QUE ES A MI CARGO, EN LA FOJA NUMERO _____ 04 _____ SE ENCUENTRA ASENTADA EL ACTA NUM. _____ 04 _____ LEVANTADA POR EL OFICIAL DEL REGISTRO DEL ESTADO FAMILIAR _____

_____ P.D.D. JUAN HERNANDEZ CHIAPA. _____

EN _____ ATOTONILCO EL GRANDE, HIDALGO, 10 DE ENERO DE 1996. _____

(LUGAR Y FECHA)

LA CUAL CONTIENE LOS SIGUIENTES DATOS:

ACTA DE MATRIMONIO

CONTRAYENTES

NOMBRE DEL CONTRAYENTE ████████ ████████ ████████ _____ EDAD _____ 30

LUGAR DE NACIMIENTO _____ JALTEPEC, TULANCINGO, HIDALGO. _____ NACIONALIDAD _____ MEXICANA

NOMBRE DE LA CONTRAYENTE _____ MARIA GUADALUPE BARRON PEREZ _____ EDAD _____ 18

LUGAR DE NACIMIENTO _____ TULPETLAC, ESTADO DE MEXICO. _____ NACIONALIDAD _____ MEXICANA

PADRES DEL CONTRAYENTE

NOMBRE DEL PADRE _____ ████████████████ _____ NACIONALIDAD _____ MEXICANA

NOMBRE DE LA MADRE _____ ████████████████ _____ NACIONALIDAD _____ MEXICANA

PADRES DE LA CONTRAYENTE

NOMBRE DEL PADRE _____ ████████████ (FINADO) NACIONALIDAD _____ MEXICANA

NOMBRE DE LA MADRE _____ ████████████ _____ NACIONALIDAD _____ MEXICANA

TESTIGOS DE LOS CONTRAYENTES

NOMBRE ████████████ _____ EDAD _____ 31 _____ NACIONALIDAD _____ MEXICANA

NOMBRE ████████████ Z _____ EDAD _____ 60 _____ NACIONALIDAD _____ MEXICANA

NOMBRE ████████████ _____ EDAD _____ 41 _____ NACIONALIDAD _____ MEXICANA

NOMBRE ████████████ _____ EDAD _____ 32 _____ NACIONALIDAD _____ MEXICANA

NOMBRE(S) DE LAS PERSONA(S) QUE DA(N) SU CONSENTIMIENTO POR MINORIA DE EDAD DE (LOS) CONTRAYENTE(S):

AUTORIZACION DE LA SECRETARIA DE GOBERNACION EN EL CASO DE CONTRAYENTE(S) ESTRANJERO(S):

ESTE CONTRATO DE MATRIMONIO ESTA SUJETO AL REGIMEN DE:

SOCIEDAD CONYUGAL ⊗   SEPARACION DE BIENES ○

SE EXTIENDE ESTA CERTIFICACION, EN CUMPLIMIENTO DEL ARTICULO 386 DEL CODIGO FAMILIAR VIGENTE EN EL ESTADO, EN _____ ATOTONILCO EL GRANDE, HIDALGO. _____

A LOS _____ 11 _____ DIAS DEL MES DE _____ ABRIL _____ DE _____ 2001.

SELLO DE LA OFICIALIA DEL REGISTRO DEL ESTADO FAMILIAR

ABOUT THE AUTHOR

Brian D. Lerner is an Immigration Lawyer and runs a National Immigration Law Firm for nearly 30 years. He is an attorney who is a certified specialist that might help in Immigration & Nationality Law as issued by the California State Bar, Board of Legal Specialization. Attorney Lerner is an expert in Immigration Law, Removal and Deportation, Citizenship, Waiver and Appeals.

He has been a licensed attorney since 1992 and started the Law Offices of Brian D. Lerner, APC. The immigration practice consists of Immigration and Nationality Law, and everything involved with and regarding immigration which includes citizenship, investment visas, family and employment visas, removal and deportation hearings, appeals, waivers, adjustment, consulate processing and all types of immigration and citizenship matters.

He has represented clients from all over the U.S. and in many countries around the world. One side of his practice is dedicated to keeping people in the U.S. and fighting for their immigration rights, while another side is to get people back who have been deported and removed from the U.S.

Also, there is the affirmative part of Immigration Law which Brian Lerner has helped numerous people come into the U.S. on business visas, investment visas, student visas, fiancée and marriage visas, religious visas and many more. Attorney Lerner has helped immigrants who are victims of crime and domestic violence or ones that are married to abusers.

In other words, Attorney Lerner has a firm that helps people all over the U.S. He has dedicated significant time to preparing numerous petitions and applications for you to get at a fraction of the price of hiring an attorney. He says it is the next best thing to a real attorney because they are real petitions prepared by an expert.

37

www.ingramcontent.com/pod-product-compliance
Lightning Source LLC
Chambersburg PA
CBHW051802200326

41597CB00025B/4651